<u>INDEX</u>

Corbyn: Leader of Labour Party

The Labour Party undoubtedly moved to the left under Ed Miliband's leadership, perhaps to a greater extent than the Westminster media and political establishment realized at the time.

Labour's new intake of MPs in 2015 is regarded as the most left-leaning in 20 years while the party's position on a range of issues - from welfare to Europe - is unrecognizable from its New Labour heyday, a fact acknowledged by Tony Blair. An estimated 70% of those who voted in the contest have joined Labour since 2010.

But it was a surge in popularity of grassroots campaigns outside the Labour Party that may have proved more decisive in the rise of Jeremy Corbyn. The People's Assembly Against Austerity, which was launched in 2013, backed by trade unions, CND, the Communist Party and Mr Corbyn himself, drew large crowds at meetings and marches across the UK.

High profile speakers such as comedian Russell Brand and columnist Owen Jones caught the imagination of young, social-media savvy activists hungry for social change. Mr Corbyn also benefitted from the formidable organisational skills of his trade union backers - something the other candidates could not, or in the case of Andy Burnham who distanced himself from the unions - would not emulate.

The rise of the anti-austerity movement would have had a minimal impact on the Labour leadership contest but for one crucial factor. The change in Labour's leadership contest rules in 2014 was heralded as a way of reducing the influence of the trade unions but it also allowed anyone to take part in ballots for a £3 fee.

It received little attention at the time but nearly 200,000 people have taken advantage of it. This appears to have caught Jeremy Corbyn's leadership rivals, who focused their message on the existing Labour membership, by surprise. Only Mr Corbyn had a link to the £3 affiliate scheme on his campaign website. Panic spread through the party when mischievous Conservative supporters started claiming they had signed up for a vote to sabotage the contest.

A different kind of panic took hold when it emerged that supporters of other parties, most notably the Greens but also far left groups, were attempting to sign up. There was much talk of "entryism" and a purge by party officials, which saw more than 3,000 people banned from casting a ballot because they were deemed not to support Labour's "aims and values".

Only Mr Corbyn, of the three candidates fully embraced the new arrivals (apart from the Conservatives of course), promising them a role in setting Labour's policy agenda.

Jeremy Corbyn surprised many people when he entered the race weeks after his rivals, in a low-key announcement to the Islington Tribune. At the time it was generally assumed he could not possibly win, with commentators describing him variously as a "maverick", "Caracas Corbyn" and a member of the "loony left", suggesting that he was trying to make a point rather than get elected.

He would not even have been a candidate in the first place if it hadn't been for the generosity of some of his fellow MPs. Under the contest's rules, he needed the support of 35 MPs - 20% of the parliamentary party - to be nominated and to get onto the ballot paper. This looked unlikely as he hovered around the 30 mark close to the deadline in mid-June.

Yet, he managed to get over the threshold with minutes to spare. The reason he did so was that a number of MPs - including some with diametrically opposed views - "lent" him their votes. At the time, they argued Labour needed the widest possible debate after its election defeat and it would be wrong if the left of the party was excluded.

Those MPs who helped Mr Corbyn over the line were memorably derided by John McTernan, ex-adviser to Tony Blair, as "*morons who need to have their heads felt*". One of them, former acting party leader Margaret Beckett, ruefully owned up to being a "moron".

Jeremy Corbyn's task was undoubtedly made easier by the absence of heavy-hitting rivals. The pool of potential opponents had already been reduced by Labour's election losses while senior figures within the party - including deputy leader Harriet Harman and former home secretary Alan Johnson - quickly ruled themselves out of the contest.

The party's "next generation" - those elected in 2010 and since - also largely decided to sit out the fight with Chuka Umunna's decision to quit the race after only a couple of days symptomatic of their tentativeness. Dan Jarvis, a former soldier who was much touted as a future leader, also declined to take part.

With two of Mr Corbyn's opponents - Andy Burnham and Yvette Cooper - having served in the Cabinet under Gordon Brown and also having been close allies of Ed Miliband and the third, Liz Kendall, tagged as the "Blairite" candidate, Mr Corbyn was able to associate his rivals with the erosion of Labour support during the past decade and argue effectively that only he offered a true break from the recent past.

There may have been a record number of campaign hustings but few of them captured the public imagination. In contrast, Jeremy Corbyn's public appearances drew crowds that few politicians can dare to dream of. Thousands flocked to events up and down the country to hear him speak. First, it was standing room only, then people found themselves being turned away - with the candidate at one point addressing hundreds of people in a London street while standing on top of a fire engine.

This was more than an inkling of how Corbynmania had energised the previously lacklustre campaign. Although 20 years older than his rivals, his ability to appeal to idealistic young people, excited by his anti-austerity message and rejection of decades-long orthodoxies, also took the Westminster establishment by surprise and marked him out from his opponents.

In an era of sharp suits and sharper haircuts, Jeremy Corbyn immediately stood out from the crowd. His slightly ruffled trademark vest and shirt combination - he was rarely seen wearing a jacket or tie during the campaign - may have been mocked by Private Eye but it gave him an authenticity and distinctiveness rare in modern politics.

Jeremy Corbyn, whose small but select group of advisers is led by former Ken Livingstone aide Simon Fletcher, also remained unruffled on the campaign trail, eschewing soundbites and refraining from personal attacks while his opponents' briefed against each other.

He avoided stunts and - apart from a few testy exchanges, most memorably on Channel 4 News and BBC Radio 4's The World at One - he handled the unaccustomed media scrutiny well. There will be plenty more to come no doubt

Minutes after his victory, Corbyn said the message is that people are *"fed up with the injustice and the inequality"* of Britain.

"The media and many of us, simply didn't understand the views of young people in our country. They were turned off by the way politics was being conducted. We have to and must change that. The fightback gathers speed and gathers pace," he said.

The north London MP is one of the most unexpected winners of the party leadership in its history, after persuading Labour members and supporters that the party needed to draw a line under the New Labour era of Blair and Gordon Brown.

Attention will now turn to who serves in Corbyn's top team, with MPs such as John McDonnell, Angela Eagle, Sadiq Khan, Ken Livingstone and possibly leadership rival Burnham tipped for key roles. Liam Byrne, Mary Creagh and John Healey have also indicated they would be willing to serve on his frontbench.

He faces the task of constructing a broad-based shadow cabinet, pulling out of his major TV interview with Andrew Marr on the BBC on Sunday to start the process. However, within two hours it was clear that Rachel Reeves, Emma Reynolds, Tristram Hunt, Chris Leslie and Liz Kendall as well as Cooper would not serve his leadership. Jamie Reed, a shadow health minister, published his resignation letter on Twitter while Corbyn was still delivering his victory speech.

Having been catapulted from a little-known member of parliament to leader of the opposition, Corbyn will now set about apologising for the Iraq war and strongly opposing cuts to public services and welfare. He began his leadership on Saturday with a speech to a rally in London in support of refugees.

Addressing the party's new members who helped propel him to victory, he said: *"Welcome to our party, welcome to our movement. And I say to those returning to the party, who were in it before and felt disillusioned and went away: welcome back, welcome home."*

Corbyn also launched a forthright attack on the media, saying its behaviour had been at times "intrusive, abusive and simply wrong". *"I say to journalists: attack public political figures. That is ok but please don't attack people who didn't ask to be put in the limelight. Leave them alone in all circumstances,"* he said.

In generous tributes to the other candidates, he applauded Burnham for his work on health, Kendall for her friendship during the campaign and Cooper for helping to shape the political narrative on Britain taking more refugees.

Winning 59.5 percent of the ballot in the first round — more than the half required — left Corbyn the clear victor, and negated the need for a second round of voting. "Yes we did!" chanted his supporters as the new leader took the stage at a special party conference in London. In his victory speech, Corbyn called for a "decent and better society" and urged party unity.

He hailed *"our party and our movement, passionate, democratic, diverse, united and absolutely determined in our quest for a decent and better society that is possible for all."*

He also condemned "grotesque levels of inequality" and "an unfair welfare system" and called for the Conservative government to show more "compassion" in dealing with the Syrian refugee crisis, saying he would attend a demonstration planned in London.

Corbyn said Labour was *"united and absolutely determined in our quest for a decent and better society that is possible for all."*

The battle-hardened, bearded MP who has stood for London's Islington North constituency since 1983, is known neither as an inspiring orator nor a charismatic leader, but projects the image of a humble man who travels by bicycle and cultivates his own garden.

Corbyn's background

Corbyn was born in 1949 to a middle-class family. His mother was a teacher and his father an engineer, and they reportedly met while campaigning on the Spanish civil war.

As a teenager, he became involved in causes such as the Campaign for Nuclear Disarmament, and both Corbyn and his elder brother joined the Young Socialists. Corbyn did not finish his studies at the North London Polytechnic. He was elected to Haringey Council, a municipal authority in north London, in 1974 at 25.

He served as a full time trade union organizer before he entered the House of Commons as lawmaker for London's Islington North in 1983 — a seat he has held ever since. Corbyn has been a fixture at left-leaning demonstrations for decades.

In 1984, he was arrested outside the South African Embassy in London for protesting against apartheid. As a long-time nuclear disarmament campaigner, he opposes the renewal of Britain's Trident nuclear fleet. In 2001 he helped establish the Stop the War coalition to campaign against the war in Iraq — and he still remains the group's chair.

Corbyn is patron of the Palestine Solidarity Campaign and takes a keen interest in championing "the rights of the oppressed" around the world, according to his website.

Britain's center-right newspaper, the Daily Telegraph, has repeatedly noted that in 1984 Corbyn invited Gerry Adams, longtime leader of the Irish nationalist Sinn Fein party and reputedly a former Irish Republican Army commander, to the House of Commons days after a deadly IRA bombing in England.

More recently Corbyn faced a television grilling when an interviewer questioned whether he called the militant groups Hamas and Hezbollah "friends." Corbyn replied that he used the word in a "collective way" and did not agree with the actions of the two groups. But he said he believed "you have to talk to people with whom you may profoundly disagree" to bring about a peace process.

Corbyn has long been known as a Labour rebel — he has voted to defy party whips for over 500 times. Within Britain, Corbyn wants to scrap university tuition fees and introduce laws to bring railways into public control. He wants to abandon economic austerity in favor of printing money to build affordable homes and other infrastructure.

Corbyn has stressed the need for what he called "tax justice" — "those with the most, pay the most" — and argues for cracking down on tax avoidance and evasion by businesses and the wealthy. Abroad, Corbyn believes Britain should consider pulling out of NATO, wants Britain to spend less on defense and is against air strikes in Syria.

Jeremy Corbyn has been addressing increasingly sizeable audiences across the country, enthusing young new voters and Labour veterans alike with his anti-austerity, leftwing message declaring that the current economic and political status quo is neither inevitable nor desirable.

This stands in stark contrast to his rivals in the contest to succeed Ed Miliband, the Labour leader who presided over a huge loss for his party at the election in May. Corbyn's fellow candidates Andy Burnham, Yvette Cooper and Liz Kendall are struggling to convince potential voters that their moderate policies are what the party needs to win back power from the Conservatives in five years' time.

Meanwhile, senior Labour figures have warned of the "madness" of a Jeremy Corbyn-led party. The former Labour prime minister Tony Blair, who led the party to three election victories, had a simple message to those whose heart was being swayed by Corbyn: "Get a transplant."

Corbyn is not a sexy politician. Member of parliament for a north London constituency since 1983, he is neither a fresh new face on the national scene, nor a striking orator with a magnetic presence. This is not Britain's Alexis Tsipras. He is an understated, thoughtful politician, happier to talk policy or discuss the people behind him than to focus on his own personal importance. Age 63, bearded and soft-spoken, Corbyn has attracted mocking headlines for his beige clothing and vests bought from the local market.

Nevertheless, he stands out from the other candidates. Burnham, Cooper and Kendall are seen by many Corbyn supporters as the same type of bland, technocratic and interchangeable career politician that puts people off from getting involved in politics, or even voting at all.

While his rivals desperately try to triangulate a centrist position that will satisfy both the party base and hypothetical voters of the kind they think Labour would need to win to gain power, Corbyn calls for renationalisation of the railways and energy companies, measures to address a burgeoning housing crisis, and increased public investment in banks, infrastructure, education and health. He also offers policies for a younger generation left reeling by cuts to education and welfare.

Some sections of the rightwing British media have barely been able to contain their glee at Corbyn's rise, with the Daily Telegraph even openly encouraging their readers to sign up as Labour supporters to vote him in as leader, in the expectation that his leadership would lead the party to electoral doom or even to the demise of the party.

Certainly a Corbyn victory would cause tensions within the party: he very much reflects the small section of the party that has refused to accept the neoliberal consensus. He only made it on to the ballot because some politicians felt they should vote for him, despite disagreeing with him, in order to ensure a wide debate. Some of them may be regretting this now.

There are, broadly speaking, two schools of thought on what Jeremy Corbyn represents. One remains very popular with media commentators: that he represents a hysterical and childish response from the British left who, thoroughly rejected in May's general election, have responded by turning to someone even less likely to be elected; in short, that they are wallowing in the comfort of opposition. Serious figures like the Guardian's columnist Polly Toynbee have warned that Jeremy Corbyn as leader would be political suicide at a time when the country needs a strong and electable opposition to Conservative cuts.

The other is that after an election in which voters struggled to differentiate between the positions of the three main parties in England, and voted in huge numbers for an anti-austerity nationalist party in Scotland, Corbyn at least represents a jolt to the status quo. Some 60,000 new members have signed up to join Labour since May's election, and among the returning members are thousands of people who have never taken an interest in politics before.

Like Bernie Sanders in the US, Corbyn is a reminder that voters today seem to crave authenticity and a challenge to to the status quo – even if, in the final analysis, that may not necessarily be an electable one.

Jews' fear

And while British Jews have expressed alarm over what they say are his somewhat dubious ties, Corbyn has hit back at criticism for his associations with pro-Palestinian figures who have espoused anti-Semitic views.

A senior Jewish member of the Labour Party said in August that Corbyn's views are cause for "serious concern." Ivan Lewis, the shadow, or minority, party cabinet minister who is also a former chief executive of the Manchester Jewish Federation, urged his party not to vote for Corbyn.

"Some of [Corbyn's] stated political views are a cause for serious concern," Lewis said in letter to his local party members on Friday, according to the Guardian. *"At the very least he has shown very poor judgment in expressing support for and failing to speak out against people who have engaged not in legitimate criticism of Israeli governments but in anti-Semitic rhetoric."*

Last month, Britain's top Jewish newspaper, the Jewish Chronicle, claimed that Corbyn, who has ties to the Socialist Campaign Group, Amnesty International and the Campaign for Nuclear Disarmament, was linked to "Holocaust deniers, terrorists and some outright anti-Semites."

"We are certain that we speak for the vast majority of British Jews in expressing deep foreboding at the prospect of Mr. Corbyn's election as Labour leader," the newspaper editorialized.

Corbyn, who six years ago offered to host representatives of Hamas and Hezbollah in the British Parliament, attempted to clarify his position in a July interview with the British TV station Channel 4.

The new Labour leader insisted at the time that he used the word "friends" in "collective way" to describe the extremist Islamist organizations during a 2009 speech, but did not endorse their views.

"I'm saying that people I talk to, I use it in a collective way, saying our friends are prepared to talk," he said of his decision to invite representatives of the two groups to address MPs six years ago.

"Does it mean I agree with Hamas and what it does? No. Does it mean I agree with Hezbollah and what they do? No. What it means is that I think to bring about a peace process, you have to talk to people with whom you may profoundly disagree," he said.

Corbyn said he had extended an invitation to the two organizations to facilitate dialogue in the Israeli-Palestinian negotiations. *"I welcomed our friends from Hezbollah to have a discussion and a debate, and I said I wanted Hamas to be part of that debate. I have met Hamas in Lebanon and I've met Hezbollah in this country and Lebanon,"* he said.

Drawing a parallel between the ideology of the militant groups and right- wing Israeli politics, Corbyn said that he had encountered Israelis with extremist views often times attributed only to Palestinians.

"I've also had discussions with people from the right in Israeli politics who have the same view possibly that the state of Israel should extend from the river to the sea, as it is claimed people from the Palestinian side do," he said

The Foreign Ministry in Jerusalem and Israel's embassy in London refrained from publishing any response to Corbyn's victory, even though this victory will have ramifications for Labor's relationship with Israel and the UK's Jewish community.

Some in the community believe that the wealthy British Jewish establishment, which has traditionally supported Labor, may now defect to the Conservatives or a newer, centrist party. Corbyn's win is a nightmare for many of Britain's 290,000 Jews. Several years ago, a Jewish Chronicle poll showed that 70 percent of British Jews were concerned about the consequences if Corbyn was elected leader. More than 80 percent of Jews expressed concern about Corbyn's potential foreign policy and ties to Holocaust deniers.

Corbyn's election raises complex questions about the future of the British Jewish community's relationship with Labor. It's unclear whether he will become more moderate, like many politicians on the left, or maintain his positions. *The Jewish Chronicle* wrote that after five difficult years under Ed Miliband's leadership, many in the Jewish community could see his heir as someone they cannot work with.

Corbyn has already conveyed messages that he intends to appoint a special envoy for Jewish affairs to communicate with the local community. Corbyn would, if elected prime minister, initially have to deal with urgent issues like the economy and education before he could approach the Palestinian matter. However, based on his prior statements, it's likely that Corbyn will adopt a tough stance towards Israel and call for sanctions, boycotts on products from settlements and support for a Palestinian state.

In the event of a violent conflict, it's likely that he would condemn Israel, just as his predecessor did during Operation Protective Edge. But how far would he get in the Commons with anti-Israel proposals, when so many in the parliamentary Labour Party seem destined to refuse to back him on a wide range of issues?

Corbyn will face his first test as head of Labour in about eight months, when the UK has local elections. Some in the Jewish community fear that if he remains in the role until the next scheduled general election in 2020, and fails to adjust his policies, the damage to Labour's relationship with the Jewish community could be irreversible.

Corbyn managed to cause a political storm as a result of a statement in which he labeled the assassination of Osama Bin Laden a "*tragedy.*" According to the Telegraph, Corbyn's spokesman defended the remarks saying he was "a total opponent of al-Qaeda, all it stands for".

In an interview with Iran's Press TV, Corbyn described the death of Bin Laden a tragedy. According to Corbyn, "*There was no attempt whatsoever that I can see to arrest him and put him on trial, to go through that process,*" he said. "*This was an assassination attempt, and is yet another tragedy, upon a tragedy, upon tragedy."*

Many senior leaders in the party oppose Corbyn, and many – including former Labour prime ministers Tony Blair and Gordon Brown – had issued public warnings strongly urging voters to reject Corbyn, arguing that his socialist ideas will alienate moderate voters and make Labour unelectable.

Israel's *Labour Party lobby*

Corbyn's victory could also affect the *Labour Friends of Israel* organization, which once numbered some 100 MPs. The organization was led in the past by very high-ranking politicians, including Tony Blair. When Miliband headed labor, the organization dropped to about 50-60 MPs.

The new chairman of Labour Friends of Israel has acknowledged the *"deep concerns"* around Jeremy Corbyn's leadership campaign and urged supporters to instead back a figure who could play a key role in the Middle East peace process.

Joan Ryan was appointed to lead LFI in Parliament on Monday, replacing Anne McGuire who stood down at the general election. Ms Ryan, a former Home Office minister and party whip, was re-elected as an MP in May in the Enfield North constituency.

She pledged to tackle pro-boycott voices within Labour and said she would oppose de-legitimization of Israel. She travelled to the country with LFI last December.

Ms Ryan, who nominated Liz Kendall in the party's leadership contest, said last month's Jewish community hustings for the contenders had been a key step in the party's efforts to *"win back the trust and confidence of the Jewish community"*.

She added: *"We hope that Labour party members and supporters will consider when they vote which candidate is best placed to ensure that the next Labour government can play a constructive and engaged role in the crucial search for a two-state solution. We recognize the deep concerns which exist about positions taken, and statements made, by Jeremy Corbyn in the past and recognize the serious questions which arise from these."*

The new chair said Labour must be *"steadfast"* in its support for Israel. LFI would *"continue to work with progressives in both Israel and Palestine who share our commitment to peace and co-existence. At the same time, we remain adamantly opposed to boycotts and sanctions, which de-legitimise Israel, do nothing to further these goals and have no place in the Labour party."*

Ms Ryan was ousted from Parliament in 2010 following the expenses scandal but returned with a majority of more than 1,000 in May.

Deir Yassin

According to the Daily Mail, Paul Eisen blogged that the Labour leadership frontrunner was a regular at Deir Yassin Remembered (DYR) gatherings and "opened his chequebook" for the group. DYR holds an annual event commemorating the killing by Jewish soldiers of 100 Arabs before the 1948 War of Independence. In a blog written in 2012 and titled *"Why I call myself a Holocaust denier"*, Mr Eisen questioned the existence of the Nazi gas chambers, and whether Hitler planned to exterminate Europe's Jews.

But the spokesperson declined to comment when asked if Mr Corbyn had *"opened his chequebook"* for DYR and attended commemoration events. Mr Corbyn was also caught up in a controversy over Stephen Sizer, the vicar disciplined by the Church of England in February over using his website to link to conspiracy theories that Israel was responsible for 9/11.

Hamas' welcome

Hamas has hailed Jeremy Corbyn for his "sympathetic" stance on the Israel-Palestinian conflict after learning that he was a front-runner to become the next Labour leader. Senior officials with the Palestinian Islamist group, which dominates Gaza, said the Left-wing MP was a welcome contrast to other British politicians, most notably Tony Blair, whom they mistrust and accuse of blindly supporting Israel.

Their endorsement follows widespread criticism of Mr Corbyn for describing a Hamas delegation as "friends" when it visited Westminster several years ago along with members of Hizbollah, the Lebanese Shia organisation.

"I find that he has very good sympathy and support for the Palestinian cause and the Palestinian struggle and he is frankly against the occupation, against the racist policy of Israel, against settlements," said Ghazi Hamad, Hamas' deputy foreign minister, who admitted that he had never met Mr Corbyn but was judging him by his speeches and media reports.

"According to his statements, I feel that he could be very close to the Palestinians, the Arabs and to the Muslims. He supports all the right things in the world regarding freedom, justice, dignity, the right of people under occupation to get their national rights. If he really became the head of the Labour party, he can make a big change to the image of Britain because people here in Palestine feel that Britain has a historical responsibility, in giving Israel the golden chance of establishing their state on the account of the Palestinian people."

Many Palestinians blame Britain for the establishment of Israel because of the 1917 Balfour Declaration that paved the way for a Jewish homeland in historic Palestine and for subsequent British policy when it ruled the territory under an international mandate.

Mr Hamad stopped short of saying that the group would regard Mr Corbyn as a friend if he were elected. *" In order to be careful, I don't want this word to be used against him,"* he said. *"But we expect him to translate what he said before into actions - to move from words to deeds. We expect Mr Corbyn and Britain to change the policy and to understand that the struggle of the Palestinian people against the occupation is fair. And that Hamas is not a terrorist organisation. This can prove that he really can be a good friend for the Palestinians. I expect that Israel will take some measures against him and try to distort his image, to destroy him. They want to show that Hamas is an animal with two horns, a dragon. So I hope that Mr Corbyn will have more courage to meet these challenges and to stand against the Israeli campaign against him."*

Mr Corbyn, the MP for Islington North, has called for the lifting of the blockade of the Gaza Strip, which has been in force since 2006, a trade and investment embargo on Israeli settlements, an end to the occupation of the West Bank, and a "right of return" for Palestinian refugees, something Israel vehemently opposes.

He insists talking to Hamas - regarded by the United States and Israel as a terrorist group - is essential to resolving the decades old Israeli-Palestinian conflict. He has said he used the word "friends" in a collective way when referring to Hamas and that it did not mean he agreed with the group or its policies. But supporters of Israel have cited it as evidence of his perceived hostility to the Jewish state.

Israel and Hamas have fought three wars since 2009, including a devastating 50-day conflict last summer that killed more than 2,200 Palestinians - the majority of them civilians - and 73, on the Israeli side, mostly soldiers.

Despite Mr Corbyn's friendly rhetoric, no leading Hamas figures recall having met him, or even having been familiar with him before he emerged as a leadership candidate. Mr Hamad initially confused him with Sir Jeremy Greenstock, the former British ambassador to the United Nations, who has also called for negotiations with Hamas. Nevertheless, Mr Hamad said Mr Corbyn could be invited to visit the coastal enclave - home to 1.8 million mostly impoverished Palestinians - if he became Labour leader. "*I think he will be welcomed. All the people would welcome him,*" he said. "*According to his vision, I think people will find that they can find some common background with him, that they can talk to him.*"

Ahmed Yousef, a confidant of Ismail Haniya, the Hamas leader in Gaza, said Mr Corbyn's statements showed him as "a man of conscience". "*Unfortunately most of the world leaders are not supporting Gaza or lack the courage to say certain things like this guy Jeremy,*" he said. "*It's not a matter of supporting or not supporting, or being a friend or not a friend. He is a man of justice, who really understands the rights and wrongs.*"

The Jewish Chronicle's questions

As Leader of the Opposition, Mr Corbyn will hold a formal constitutional role, and will hold a hope — however realistic or otherwise — of becoming Prime Minister. The JC rarely claims to speak for anyone other than ourselves. We are just a newspaper. But in this rare instance we are certain that we speak for the vast majority of British Jews in expressing deep foreboding at the prospect of Mr Corbyn's election as Labour leader.

Because, although there is no direct evidence that he has an issue himself with Jews, there is overwhelming evidence of his association with, support for — and even in one case, alleged funding of — Holocaust deniers, terrorists and some outright anti-Semites.

If Mr Corbyn is not to be regarded from the day of his election as an enemy of Britain's Jewish community, he has a number of questions which he must answer in full and immediately. The JC asked him earlier to respond. No response has been forthcoming.

1. Did you donate, as alleged by its founder, to Deir Yassin Remembered (DYR), a group that publishes open anti-semitism, run by Holocaust denier Paul Eisen — an organisation so extreme that even the Palestine Solidarity Campaign refuses to associate with it?

2. Have you, as Mr Eisen claims, regularly attended DYR's annual conference?

3. Why have you accepted an invitation to appear at a conference on August 22 alongside Carlos Latuff, the notorious anti-Semitic cartoonist?

4. Why did you write to the Church of England authorities to defend Rev Stephen Sizer, a vicar banned from social media because of his habit of posting anti-Semitic conspiracy theories, telling them that Rev Sizer was "under attack" because he had "dared to speak out over Zionism"?

5. Why do you associate with Hamas and Hezbollah and refer to them as your "friends"?

6. Why have you failed to condemn the anti-Semitic posters and banners that dominate the annual Al-Quds Day rally, sponsored by the Stop The War Coalition, which you chair?

7. Why did you describe Raead Salah, a man convicted of the blood libel, as an 'honoured citizen'?

It is difficult not to see a pattern in Mr Corbyn's associations, and his refusal at any point to answer the fears of the Jewish community raised by these associations.

In a nation where, thank heavens, racism and extremism are now regarded as beyond the pale, it is little short of astonishing that a man who chooses to associate with racists and extremists is about to become leader of one of our two main parties and could conceivably become Prime Minister.

Corbyn: About Israel

Jeremy Corbyn: I have never heard Israel declare what its final frontiers ought to be. In every negotiation, it refuses to say what its borders ought to be. ...

Jeremy Corbyn: There are two points. First, Israel fails to say what its final borders are. Secondly, Israel did deal with Hamas in the ceasefire negotiations in Egypt. There is a basis on which talks can take place. It has already happened.

...

Jeremy Corbyn: I start my contribution by thanking all the people who signed this e-petition and other petitions to ensure that the debate would take place, and all the people who have campaigned not just for months but for years for the recognition of a Palestinian state and justice for the Palestinian people. Those who have stood on wet and windy high streets on a Saturday morning collecting signatures do matter in a democracy, and this debate is, in a sense, the product of that.

In the short time available to me, I want to draw attention to a few points. First, I was asked to give a talk last week to a group of students at City and Islington College about the history of the whole conflict in the Middle East. It was a fascinating discussion, which ranged from the First World War right up to the current situation. The students had an incredible sense of the historical importance of the vote that took place in Parliament recently, when we voted finally for the recognition of Palestine, but I argue very strongly that that is only one very small step that we need to take.

A settlement has to involve an awful lot more than just the recognition of the state of Palestine. People should cast their minds back to Sabra and Shatila in 1982 and to the Nakba in 1948. The victims of those processes are still living in refugee camps in Lebanon, Jordan and Syria; the Palestinian diaspora across the world is huge. They also have rights—they also have the right to return home and a right to recognition. That is extremely important. They should never be forgotten.

Secondly, any peace process requires Israel to say what it wishes its final borders to be. My hon. Friend the Member for East Kilbride, Strathaven and Lesmahagow (Mr McCann) made many points, as did others, about the Hamas charter and what it is supposed to say. The reality is that Hamas is involved in a unity Government, and that is what provoked Operation Protective Edge this summer.

Jeremy Corbyn: Absolutely. The Likud charter, which is not talked about too much by those who support the Government of Israel, says that in those very specific terms, and there has to be some recognition that the Prime Minister of Israel is a member of Likud and is in power because of Likud support.

Another point—there are many—is that half a million people are now settlers all across the west bank. Travelling around the west bank is travelling through an occupied land where the best land and the best water are taken by the settlers, the red-roofed buildings are built increasingly over Palestinian land and the massive concrete wall snakes around the place. If it was unwrapped, so to speak, it would stretch all across Europe.

That wall divides farmers from their land, divides people from their water, divides children from their schools and makes travelling impossible. There has to be not just an end to the settlement policy but an end to the settlements. They have to go; they have to be withdrawn if there is to be any peace settlement.

Another issue is, of course, trade. Britain is a trading partner of Israel. We sell arms to Israel; we buy arms from Israel. Although some licences have been suspended or withdrawn, the arms trade goes on. If we are making engines for drone aircraft in this country and those drones are used for surveillance over

Gaza and used to bomb the people of Gaza, as they were during Operation Protective Edge, we are complicit in what goes on there.

That is what provoked an awful lot of people to sign the petition and make their views heard recently. Gaza is under siege and has been under siege for a very long time. It has been my pleasure to visit Gaza on nine separate occasions during the past 15 years or so, and there is a feeling of depression and anger there at the way in which the people of Gaza are denied the right to work, the right to travel, the right to trade and the right to develop. Now, Egypt is joining in with that by developing a cordon sanitaire along the border between Egypt and Gaza, so I hope that when the Minister replies, we will hear some fairly robust remarks about the policies being followed by Egypt at present, which are compounding the siege of Gaza already being undertaken by Israel. A powder keg is developing because of the lack of freedom to travel, the lack of supplies, the lack of water and the lack of food. The people are crying out for recognition, help and support.

Jeremy Corbyn: May I take the Foreign Secretary back to his favourite subject, a nuclear weapons-free middle east? That has now become a greater possibility with an interim agreement with Iran. Will he update us on progress on a conference that would include Israel, which of course is the only country in the region that has declared nuclear weapons?

Corbyn: 2020

The controversy in Labour circles about Jeremy Corbyn centres on the issue of whether or not he is electable as prime minister. While there are divisions about policy, all Labour members are signed up to his broad goals of social justice, equality and peace, but there is profound disagreement about whether or not he can get the party into government.

People on both sides have very entrenched views. There is no simple way of resolving the question, but here are reflections that may shed some light on what has become the key question in British politics.

> Corbyn is happy to call himself a socialist, and no one has objected to him being called leftwing. It is not always a helpful phrase, however, and his supporters have objected to him being described as far left because it implies he is extreme, and at the margins of public opinion. In some respects he probably is, but in others he isn't. His support for expansionary economic policies has more mainstream support than is commonly assumed and some of his ideas, such as nationalising the railways – a policy often dismissed as irresponsible lefty wishful thinking – have overwhelming popular support.

> The Blairite rule that Labour loses general elections when it heads left has generally been true in recent years, but Ken Livingstone offers Corbyn some hope, as he said himself this morning. Dismissed as being on the lunatic fringe, he won two elections as London mayor and ran the capital very effectively.It is interesting to speculate on what would have happened if Corbyn had stood for the mayoral nomination. While his chances of becoming prime minister may seem remote, given the

support he is attracting now, if he had entered that contest he would probably be a dead cert to replace

It would be wrong to say there is a consensus about why Labour lost the election, but there is quite a lot of evidence to suggest that a huge problem, in England and Wales at least, was that voters did not support the party on the economy, immigration or welfare. Tim Bale, another academic, has said the choice facing political parties ultimately boils down to "a choice between 'preference shaping' [the heroic assumption that you can get voters to see things your way] and 'preference accommodation' [the assumption that you need to meet them halfway]." Corbyn's victory can be seen as Labour putting a monumental bet on preference shaping. It can work but, as Bale has pointed out, it can fail too.

A lot depends on how well a leader can change public opinion, and as yet there is little evidence that Corbyn will be a great persuader. He has, of course, had a remarkable election victory, but that does not seem to be because he has changed minds. As he has suggested himself in interviews, it is more because he became an outlet for voters fed up with the Labour establishment who had at least found a candidate who represented their views. He has shown little interest in what a Labour leader might have to say to win over voters who don't already agree with him. Indeed, his victory speech On Saturday was notable in that it contained almost nothing aimed at appealing to the classic, middle England floating voter. Asked how he could win an election with his policies, Corbyn has highlighted the large number of votes Labour could win by mobilising a leftish coalition of people who either did not register or turn out in 2015, or who voted for other progressive parties because they found Labour uninspiring.

The Tories under Michael Howard and Labour under Ed Miliband were in the situation of having individual policies that were popular, but finding it hard to capitalise on those because the party's image overall was negative. Will having Corbyn as leader make people feel more positive about Labour generally? It is far too soon to know, but as yet there is no evidence that it will. There were at least two state-of-the-party polls conducted after Corbyn became the frontrunner in the leadership race, and they both show it languishing well behind the Tories – on 31 points and 28 points respectively.

The wider public beyond the nearly 500,000 people who voted in the leadership election have probably not yet formed a settled view on Corbyn. There are some aspects of his character, however, that people are likely to find very appealing. He is the antithesis of a career politician - in fact, it would be hard to find a politician less careerist – he doesn't speak in politico-cliche about hard-working families and he is self-effacing, modest and frugal.

Corbyn has said he wants to run a consensual administration - more Attlee than Churchill - and perhaps he will do this effectively. Many of his colleagues, however, think he will prove temperamentally unsuited to leadership for reasons Andy McSmith set out in the Independent.

Ultimately elections are about choosing a prime minister, and even many Corbyn admirers find it hard to see him walking through the door of 10 Downing Street. That may explain why the notion that he will only be a caretaker leader is so widespread. In his excellent account of the Corbyn campaign, my colleague Ewen MacAskill says that if Corbyn was ever minded to think this way, he has changed during the campaign, and is now "in for the long haul".

The most obvious example would be some sort of economic catastrophe, which could lead to Corbyn-led Labour defying the pundits and taking power in the manner of Syriza in Greece. It does not seem probable, but it is by no means unthinkable.

So, overall, is Corbyn really unelectable? Quite possibly, but no one can plausibly say yes or no with certainty, and ultimately only the electorate can provide the answer.To be fair, it is also worth pointing out that there are strong grounds for thinking that Corbyn's three Labour leadership rivals would also have had considerable difficulties winning the next general election.